ANR

The Butterfly Project

A Collection of Mental Health Themed Poems

First published by The Book Lover Publishing 2020

Copyright © 2020 by ANR

All rights reserved. No part of this publication may be reproduced, stored or transmitted in any form or by any means, electronic, mechanical, photocopying, recording, scanning, or otherwise without written permission from the publisher. It is illegal to copy this book, post it to a website, or distribute it by any other means without permission.

ANR asserts the moral right to be identified as the author of this work.

ANR has no responsibility for the persistence or accuracy of URLs for external or third-party Internet Websites referred to in this publication and does not guarantee that any content on such Websites is, or will remain, accurate or appropriate.

Designations used by companies to distinguish their products are often claimed as trademarks. All brand names and product names used in this book and on its cover are trade names, service marks, trademarks and registered trademarks of their respective owners. The publishers and the book are not associated with any product or vendor mentioned in this book. None of the companies referenced within the book have endorsed the book.

For additional information:

The Book Lover Publishing

main.thebooklover@gmail.com

thebooklover.cc

ANR

contact@anrofficial.com

anrofficial.com

First edition

ISBN: 979-8-64-431565-9

This book was professionally typeset on Reedsy.
Find out more at reedsy.com

To my mamaw, thank you for understanding.

Butterflies can't see their wings. They can't see how truly beautiful they are. People are like that too.

> Unknown

Contents

1	Bear a Smile	1
2	How to Admit I'm Broken	2
3	Headache	3
4	Blinking	4
5	Silence	5
6	Fourteen	6
7	Fine	8
8	Empire of Hurt	9
9	I Hurt Myself	10
10	If My Body is a Temple	12
11	A Slave to Broken Dreams	14
12	I'm Fine	16
13	Drowning	17
14	Can't Help Me	19
15	Atlas	20
16	What it's Like at the Bottom of Hell	22
17	Best Years of My Life	23
18	The Scars That remain	25
19	You Think...	26
20	Don't Want to Be You	27
21	Please Don't Leave Me	28
22	Unnoticed	30
23	Let You Down	31
24	What I'm Not	32

25	Bathroom	33
26	No Good for You	35
Mental Health information		37
About the Author		39

1

Bear a Smile

I was stranded out and I was cold,
   walked through Hell all on my own.
   And still, I managed to bear a smile...
   Once again, I was all alone,
   stuck out in the combat zone.
   And still, I laughed all the while...
   Beat me down and cause a bruise,
   say my tears are because of you.
   But really, they're tears of joy...
   Tell me what I need to do,
   give me a list, and spit on me too.
   And still, my soul, you won't destroy...
   I was stranded out and I was cold,
   walked through Hell all on my own.
   And still, I managed to bear a smile...

2

How to Admit I'm Broken

Someone give me a moment,
    teach me how to admit that I'm broken,
    that the pieces are what I own and,
    Give me time...
    To free my mind...
    Oh, can you just give me space please,
    tell me how to let my mind ease,
    and myself some granted peace...
    Oh how can I...
    Be alright...?
    Oh someone give me a moment,
    teach me how to admit that I'm broken.
    Give me the space I rightfully own and,
    Give me time...
    To be alright...

3

Headache

I know I shouldn't do this, take so many pills.
   But it hurts so bad, I just wonder if I'm ill.
   I heard an old saying, if looks could kill.
   I look in the mirror just to see if it's real.
   I'm not living for myself,
   just for everyone else.
   But I'm tired of this headache deep in my brain,
   take it all away, I just can't take this pain.
   Oh, I know I shouldn't do this, it isn't good.
   But it hurts so bad, I wonder if I should.
   I heard an old saying about a wolf,
   and I like to play dress-up, if only I could...
   Make this headache go away, deep in my brain,
   baby take it all away, wash it out with the rain.
   I'm not living for myself,
   just for everyone else.
   So maybe I'll take two,
   of the pills off the shelf...

4

Blinking

You stare while I'm blinking,
    but don't tell me what you're thinking.
    You keep staring at me,
    just don't tell me what you see.
    Do you see my demons?
    Or do you ignore them even?
    Ooh you stare while I'm blinking,
    just don't tell me what you see...

Silence

I sit in silence
   because it's all I have.
   Silence is not the lack of sound.
   It is a madness that takes over a person.
   Silence is a character trait.
   So to the girl who sits in silence
   embracing the probability of death
   with open arms:
   You are not the only silenced being.

6

Fourteen

She's only fourteen,
　so young and yet so old.
　The pain she carries
　from lifetime before turns her cold.
　Her boyfriend begs her
　not to cut into herself.
　But at the end of the day she
　ain't got nobody else.
　But the knife in her hand,
　dug deep in her thigh.
　She wonders if God has left her,
　and she begins to cry.
　She's only fourteen,
　she's got all this time.
　And still she wasted it on being sad,
　waste it on her cries.
　If only she could see
　what ever else does.
　Maybe then she'd finally

FOURTEEN

think that she was enough.
And you know this girl,
you know her so well.
Because you pushed her down in the hallway,
that's why she cuts herself.
So when the news finally comes
that she cut too deep,
and there was too much blood lost,
may she rest in peace...

Fine

I wanted to talk about it,
   I wanted to scream from the rooftops,
   I wanted people to know,
   that I felt I'd been abandoned by God.
   When they asked how I was,
   I wanted to tell the truth,
   I wanted to shout it at them.
   But at the end of the day, when they asked how I was,
   all I could do,
   is whisper,
   "I'm fine."

8

Empire of Hurt

My empire of hurt
   turned and said to me,
   "You've got all this dirt
   in your wounds where you cut and bleed."

I turned back to them
   and asked them how they know
   they said, "It's a secret,
   we'll tell you when it snows."

So I laid back on down
   on my bed of secrets and lies
   and thought about this town
   this town of my demise

But my empire of hurt
   well they woke me again
   they said, "We know why there's dirt
   because you hit rock bottom again."

9

I Hurt Myself

I hurt myself
  today
  to see how much
  I bleed
  does that scare you
  away
  the monster inside
  of me?
  oh, I hurt deep down
  inside
  from the words the bullies
  scream
  does that make you
  cry
  to see how mean they are
  to me?
  but I hurt myself
  today
  to see how much

I HURT MYSELF

I bleed
is that what scares you
away
this loneliness
inside of me?

10

If My Body is a Temple

I feel so alone,
    maybe I'm supposed to, I just don't know.
    I gotta home,
    but deep down inside, I'm living in the snow.

If my body's a temple,
    then this temple's haunted.
    I don't wanna be mean,
    I'm just being honest.

I feel so abandoned,
    alone and taken for granted.
    I'm not being canted,
    just tryna not to rant and...

If my body's a temple,
    then this temple's haunted.
    I don't wanna be mean,
    I'm just honest.

IF MY BODY IS A TEMPLE

And I swear to keep my one and only promise,
that if this body's a temple,
this temple's haunted...

11

A Slave to Broken Dreams

Don't you know I'm not an angel?
   I fell from Heaven at all the wrong angles.
   Chain me down and hit me real hard,
   take another piece of my of my paper heart.
   But don't give me hope for tomorrow,
   when it doesn't happen, I fill with sorrow.
   A paper girl for a paper town,
   just a paper queen without her crown.

A slave to broken dreams, I am...
   Broken dreams haunt me, again...

Don't you know I'm not an angel?
   my fall from Heaven was so fatal.
   My halo burned and I lost the ashes,
   somewhere in the past, oh I can't imagine.
   But don't look back at yesterday,
   she brings mistakes we don't wanna face.
   Pretty good at bad decisions,

A SLAVE TO BROKEN DREAMS

but I'm pretty bad without my vision.

A slave to broken dreams, I am...
   Broken dreams chain me down again...

Don't you know I'm a fallen angel,
   I fell from Heaven at all the wrong angles.
   Don't you know it was so fatal,
   my halo burns because I'm unable...
   To realize I'm a paper girl for a paper town,
   just a paper queen without her crown...

A slave to broken dreams, I am...
   Broken dreams of being an angel again...

12

I'm Fine

Today has not been a good day. No, today, I'm not bad.
  I'm fine.
  Yeah, I'm fine, all except for the pain in my chest, the burning and the feeling of not being able to breath.
  I'm fine except for the tingling feelings in my fingers, the sense of immediate danger lurking nearby.
  I'm fine, if you don't look at the fact I can't sleep, and even when I do, evading nightmares is an impossibility.
  I'm fine.
  Perfectly and completely fine.
  Let's just ignore the racing heart and numb fingers, the tight lungs, the pressure in my head, the inability to breathe.
  Lets ignore the fact that I am slowly drowning, and if we ignore it well enough, then yes,
  I am, and always be,
  fine.

13

Drowning

I know I'm clingy, I'm sorry.
   I know I tend to worry,
     I just don't want to end our story...

Hold on, I think I'm drowning...
   Don't let me go, I keep on shouting...

I know I'm jumpy, don't mean to be.
   I know my anxiety gets the best of me,
     I just don't hear you screaming...

Hold on, I think I'm drowning...
   Don't let me go, my lungs are burning...
   Don't you see my world is churning...
   And I can't keep swimming...

Hold on, I think I'm drowning,
   pull me to surface, feel my heart pounding...

Hold on, I think I'm drowning,
   tell me once again, that we're not dreaming...

14

Can't Help Me

I need help but you can't help me,
   look around, what do you see?
   Damaged goods lie around me,
   I'm sinking...

I beg for love, but turn my cheek,
   looking away from what you give me.
   It's not fair, you know I'm sorry,
   I'm sorry...

I need help but you can't help me,
   look around, what do you see?
   Bad decisions suffocate me,
   I'm sinking...

Atlas

I feel so heavy,
   like there's cement in my veins.
   This weight I can't carry,
   it hurts to hard in my brain...

If the weight of the world is on my shoulders,
   then I guess I'll shrug, and knock them over...

I feel so weak,
   like I've been stripped of my strength.
   My tears don't cease,
   just keep spilling over the brink...

If the weight of the world is on my shoulders,
   then I guess I'll shrug and knock them over...

I feel so strong!
   And yet, so weak.
   I feel so heavy!

ATLAS

And still I'm empty...

So if the weight of the world is on my shoulders,
   then I guess I'll buckle, and fall over...

16

What it's Like at the Bottom of Hell

So I say goodbye,
   telling myself it's the last time.
   I can't get hurt any more,
   they say lovers break your heart, but friends can break em' more.
   'Cause they know each and every one of your weaknesses,
   that's how she knew one of my greatest fears is abandonment.
   And she abandoned me, what's that about?
   I thought she said she'd have me through flood and through drought.
   So now as I stare at my phone,
   feeling a million miles from home,
   She left me alone,
   I've got nowhere to go.
   So I say goodbye,
   promising myself that it is alright.
   But it's not alright, no, I'm not fine.
   I'm at the bottom of Hell, someone bring me a light.

17

Best Years of My Life

I sit here thinking that this can't be real,
   this isn't what a little girl is supposed to feel.
   I sit here thinking that I am alone,
   but I'm in a middle of family and I have a home.
   Why do I feel this way, like they don't understand?
   They're sitting right here, holding onto my hand.
   I know I have friends who are here to support me,
   but I'm honestly to scared to show them the real me.
   I tell them it's been the best year of my life,
   I joined the church and now I'm being led by the Christ.
   But I feel alone on my journey, just stumbling down some path,
   hoping I chose the right one, and if not Satan will be glad.
   These dark thoughts aren't supposed to exist in my head,
   this is some horror movie crap, are there monsters under my bed?
   I'm not asking for help, actually the opposite,
   push me down, my legs are numb but I don't know how to sit.
   I don't know how to calm down, or how to chill out,

its been burned in my brain to never let down.

I've been fighting with my demons, or they've been fighting with me,

I can't tell which is wining, but they seem to always get the victory...

18

The Scars That remain

You confirmed the fear I had deep inside,
   you never really wanted to see my mind.
   You wanted my body as a toy,
   you were just like every other boy.
   When I told you of my pain,
   You brought up the rain,
   You didn't want to see the scars that remain.

I shouldn't have listened to your sweet words,
   I knew, in the end, they could cause me to hurt.
   But you had the prettiest brown eyes in town,
   there was no way that I could ever turn em' down.
   Pretty good at bad decisions and you still,
   surprised me with your wide-eyed will.
   But when I told you of my pain,
   you brought up the rain.
   You didn't want to deal with the scars that remain.

19

You Think...

You think you know me?
   You know nothing.

You think we're close?
   Close to what?

You think you've hurt me?
   You probably have.

But you think you know me?
   That's a joke.

20

Don't Want to Be You

"I love you", once more you promise,
   Come on don't lie, just be honest.
   Hit the mirror,
   In pure and utter horror...
   I don't wanna be you,
   But I always will be you...
   I don't wanna be you,
   And neither do you...

 Pull the strings, see if you break.
   Another tally mark, keep track of my mistakes.
   Hit the mirror,
   And tell it something familiar...
   I don't wanna be you,
   But I always will be you...
   I don't wanna be you,
   And neither do you...

21

Please Don't Leave Me

Please don't leave me, Is all I ever say,
   but they never seem to obey.
   Please, I can change me, I offer all day long,
   but they still walk away like I've done something wrong.
   Please, I need you,
   And still they leave me, oh it just can't be.

Please tell me the truth,
   Have I done something wrong?
   Why am I begging you all day long,
   Please don't leave me,
   I can't take it on my own.
   Oh please, I can change me,
   But once again they say its them and not me, why can't they just stay with me?

Oh please don't leave me,
   I can't fight the demons on my own.
   Please, don't leave me,

PLEASE DON'T LEAVE ME

My nights are so, so long.

Why do you leave me,
    To deal with these things on my own?

22

Unnoticed

I'm here, right in front of your eyes,
   And yet, you refuse to see me.
   I shout, begging for you to notice my weakening mind,
   and yet, you refuse to hear me.

Noticeable, and yet, unnoticed,
   I stand here, begging for your glance.

Unnoticeable, and yet noticed,
   you wave me off, without giving me a chance.
   I'm right here, in front of your very eyes,
   and still, you refuse to recognize me.

23

Let You Down

I promised I would try,
   and you thought I would.
   It wasn't a lie, I did all that I could.
   But it wasn't enough and again,
   I let you down, I let you down again,
   I let you down. I let you down again,
   I'm sorry now, again, I'm sorry now.
   Didn't mean to let you down in the end, I let you down.
   The bruises I put on you, I know it hurts.
   I cut you up all the time and so now you cry...

24

What I'm Not

I have tried so, so hard,
   to become what you are.
   You say a life is what I need,
   I don't understand; does that make me naive?
   I must've made a mistake,
   that must be why you so quickly turned away.
   I understand you're exactly what I'm not,
   but you must understand that, compared to me, you have a lot...

25

Bathroom

I locked myself in the bathroom,
   using the door as a wall you can't break through.

In my ears I can hear my heartbeat,
   but this life is nothing if you leave me.

We both fight a battle that we won't win,
   both my wrist are bleeding when you come in...
   I can feel your fingers are my neck,
   you whisper in my ear, "Don't leave me yet..."

I locked myself in the bathroom,
   trying not to sound to taboo.

In my ears I can hear my heartbeat,
   but as the blood flows just let me be.

We both fight a battle that we won't win,
   both my wrist are bleeding when you come in...

THE BUTTERFLY PROJECT

I can feel your fingers are my neck,
you whisper in my ear, "Don't leave me yet..."

26

No Good for You

You act like you're happy when I walk in the room,
   but lets not lie to each other, just tell me the truth.
   Go ahead and tell me you're scared of what I have and haven't yet to do.

Genuine fear, now most people don't know what it's like,
   but I can tell you've been there by the look in your eye.
   So I'm just sitting here wondering when you're gonna realize,

That I, I am no good for you.
   I'm gonna cause you pain, pain that you don't get used to.

Yeah you act like you're happy when you see my face,
   but let's be honest, I'm nothing but hate.
   But this isn't the kind of hate that's passionate and great.

So I, I am no good for you,
   I'm not gonna repeat myself, it's just not what I do.
   But I should let you know, I'm gonna cause you pain, pain that

you don't get used to.

So just know, that I am no good for you...

Mental Health information

Did you know...?

- 43.8 million American's adult deal with mental health disorders
- There are over 200 classified mental illness
- (According to DoSomething.org: Let's Do This!) "Members of the LGBTQ+ community are almost 3 times more likely to experience a mental health condition such as major depression or generalized anxiety disorder."
- Depression in minors has risen from 5.9% to 8.2% since 2012
- (According to the World Health Organization) Almost half of the mental health disorders bloom at age 14
- Every 40 seconds someone dies from suicide

Hotlines

- The suicide prevention hotline is: 1-800-273-8255, and is open 24/7
- The NAMI hotline is: 1-800-950-6264, and is open Monday–Friday from 10 a.m. to 6 p.m. EST
- The SAMHSA hotline is: 1-(800) 662-4357, and it too is 24/7
- The NIMH hotline is: (866) 615-6464, and is open Mon-

day–Friday, 8:30 a.m. to 5 p.m. EST.
- The Crisis Text Hotline: text CONNECT to 741741
- The Veterans Crisis Line: (phone-number) 1-800-273-8255, (text line) 838255

About the Author

ANR is a preeminent Author whose professional career began back in 2020 after her first published work, *The Butterfly Project* was released, but she's been writing since 2017. Since then, she's explored different writing genres and created a loyal group of fans who eagerly await her latest releases. With numerous bestsellers and awards to her name, ANR continues to push literary boundaries.

Coming from Lawrence County, Ohio, ANR published her first book just a week before her fifteenth birthday. Coming from a family of writers, her grandfather being the author of multiple published books, her mother is a freelance writer for their local newspaper, being a writer is just in her blood.

She has three younger sisters and two older brothers and currently lives on a homestead in Ohio, raising their six chickens, one rooster, two dogs, five rabbits, and one cat.

ANR has been volunteering at the Lawrence County Museum since she was twelve years old and does beauty pageants in her free time.

In 2017 ANR was diagnosed with depression and anxiety, both of these conditions only worsened up until the age of fifteen, where she found her outlet. As shown in some of her poetry, ANR struggles daily with her mental health and tries to portray that in her writing. She runs a mental health blog and is fixed on helping others through her work. This is why all of her poetry books are completely free, alongside the resources she has to offer.

You can connect with me on:
🌐 http://anrofficial.com

Subscribe to my newsletter:
✉ http://anrofficial.com/newsletter

Printed in Great Britain
by Amazon